Social Media and Philanthropy

A Match Made in Heaven

Table of Contents

We make a living by what we get, but we make a life by what we give.

Chapter 1. Introduction

A new dawn is emerging in the philanthropic landscape, fueled by the evolving terrain of social media. Our special report, "Social Media and Philanthropy: A Match Made in Heaven," shines a light on this compelling alliance. It is a lively and insightful exploration of how the fast-paced world of tweets, hashtags, and viral campaigns is reshaping the sphere of philanthropy, bringing change in the most incredibly interactive ways. The dance between the stalwart world of giving and the vibrant, kinetic world of social media results in a symbiotic relationship that enriches lives and communities globally. As this report unveils, it's a match made in heaven, redefining charitable actions and creating myriad opportunities for engagement and impact. This is not just another report, but a dynamic guide on how to understand and harness this powerful partnership. So, strap in and get ready to be enthralled by this electrifying evolution. This report promises to not only educate but inspire you to become part of this transformative journey. You won't resist scooping up a copy!

Chapter 2. The Dawn of Social Philanthropy

As the first light of day breaks into the darkened night sky, the dawn of social philanthropy is enlivened with an exciting chorus of digital platforms acting in concert to create meaningful impact. With social media tools at its disposal, philanthropy is transcending limitations to reach new heights.

2.1. The Advent of Social Media

The birth and rise of social media like Facebook, Twitter, Instagram, and LinkedIn immerged at the turn of the century driving profound transformation. This shift from person-to-person exchange to networking at a grand scale revolutionized numerous areas of life, and the sphere of philanthropy wasn't immune to this paradigm change. Platforms that allowed connectivity and exchange of ideas soon created an ecosystem where philanthropic mindsets could harvest generous cultures. It was crisply evident - a new dawn had arrived, one offering the gift of connectivity, communication, and collective action, decorated with the tool of social media.

2.2. The Nexus of Philanthropy and Social Media

As it became increasingly clear, social media amplifies the voice of philanthropy. But more than instant spread, it's the inherent capacity for interaction with infinitely diverse individuals, groups, organizations, and causes that distinguishes this connection. The ability to share and react to content, initiate dialogue, and build on others' perspectives breeds a vibrant culture of giving. Further, the space available within these platforms fosters an atmosphere of transparency, offering a chance to create, observe, and assess the direct result of giving mobilized through social media.

2.3. Formulation of Social Philanthropy

It didn't take long for the blend of social media's connective power and the noble intent of philanthropy to crystallize into what we now term as "social philanthropy." Here, the focus shifted from the traditionally viewed philanthropy of substantial donations from the ultra-rich to accessible, inclusive giving involving thousands, if not millions, of individuals. With broader networks, smaller, more diverse contributions started racking up, leading to significant combined effects. This phenomenon overturned the conventional wisdom that only the affluent could substantially influence change.

2.4. Principles of Social Philanthropy

Principles, based on inclusivity, transparency, collaboration, and accessibility, underlie social philanthropy. Insights into the campaigns are now readily available, and results trackable. Philanthropy expanded from selective, closed-door environments towards engagement-deep community atmospheres. Moreover, collaborative efforts found fertile soil in social media, sparking new, innovative initiatives that harness collective human action to cause ripples of changes.

2.5. Social Media: The Catalyzer of Causative Movements

Is the donation made? One retweet later, and an updated figure is available for all to view. Interested in a cause? A digital flier is just a share away from reaching hundreds, even thousands. Never before such direct access and involvement in philanthropy were available to everyone with an internet connection and a social media account. Consider crowdfunding platforms or viral challenges; social media activates a participatory model of philanthropy, igniting widespread campaigns with profound societal consequences.

2.6. The Broadening Impact of Social Philanthropy

The rise of social philanthropy trivialized the geographical barriers, and today, local initiatives can garner global support. The countless stories where campaigns go viral and aid reaches the most remote locations are powerful testaments of social philanthropy's expansive scope. They demonstrate that today, to contribute and make a difference, all you need is a sympathetic heart, an internet connection, and perhaps a hashtag or two.

As we open ourselves to this fantastic chapter of philanthropy's evolution, let us be reminded that the dawn is just the beginning. With every rising sun, we witness a new day with new opportunities to leverage social media towards a more generous, inclusive, and compassionate world. Hence, we must keep a keen eye on the horizon, enthusiastically following this evolution, utilizing these digital tools to broaden philanthropy's reach, touching more lives in more significant ways.

Chapter 3. Breaking Down Traditional Barriers in Charity

Our exploration into the transformative relationship between social media and philanthropy takes us to one fundamental aspect - how this dynamic partnership has inherently changed traditional practices in charity. The technology-fueled communication through social platforms has unlocked an astonishing potential that has dramatically shifted the paradigm of traditional charitable behaviors, solving the persistent challenges and breaking down barriers in the field. Here, we engage in a comprehensive analysis, providing an exhaustive overview of the transformative changes underway.

3.1. The Evolution of Traditional Philanthropy

Traditionally, philanthropy existed in an environment of select privileged individuals or institutions. These entities commanded the resources and the influence necessary to make a difference. They possessed enormous wealth that could be converted into philanthropic actions, often in an opaque, top-down manner. This model was not bad by design. It created countless opportunities for those in dire situations, but it inevitably fostered an exclusive environment accompanied by a lack of transparency and unequal distribution. Hence, there was an urgent need for a transformative shift - a seismic change was imperative and that was, in essence, driven by the advent of the digital era and, more specifically, social media.

3.2. Social Media: The Great Leveler

The advent of social media platforms has democratized the world of philanthropy, removing the elitism that often characterized charitable giving, and replacing it with a model that encouraged mass participation. Now, even those with modest means could make a significant impact by aligning it with a cause that resonated with them. Social media platforms like Facebook, Twitter, Instagram, LinkedIn, and YouTube, among others, have provided the much-needed platform for any individual to be a philanthropist, helping to break down the traditional view that philanthropy was the exclusive domain of the extremely wealthy.

Donations no longer have to be in the form of huge sums of money; sharing a post, being part of a campaign, volunteering in a virtual event, or engaging in online discussions all contribute to the cause. Social media has truly transformed the perception and practice of giving, making it more approachable and accessible to all.

3.3. Bridging Geographical Limitations

One of the biggest challenges of traditional philanthropy was the geographical limitations. Money, resources, and assistance often went to communities that were more accessible. The digital era, however, has torn down these boundaries. Social media platforms have connected societies on a global scale, reaching the farthest corners of the globe in a matter of seconds. This digital connection broke down geographical barriers and broadened the scope of philanthropy to a global scale. Problems half a world away are now within the scope of individuals and groups who want to make a difference.

Now, a youth in Africa can receive immediate assistance from an empathetic donor in Europe or a well-wisher in Asia within seconds of their plight being known. Consequently, charities can now raise funds for specific causes in a matter of hours or days through crowdfunding platforms integrated with these social networks. This is a profound shift in the very concept of community, from geographical locality to shared values and concerns, thus empowering the entire globe to work towards common goals.

3.4. Increasing Transparency and Trust

Another great divide in the world of traditional philanthropy was the lack of transparency. Donors often had minimal visibility about how their contributions were being utilized. This gap resulted in a lack of trust, as donors were unable to verify if their money was genuinely making an impact.

Social media has significantly altered this dynamic. In a socially connected world, charities now have a way to broadcast the impact of every dollar donated, through photos, videos, and stories, providing real-time updates and engaging donors in the cause. This form of active transparency fosters trust and intrigue, encourages further philanthropic action, provides accountability, and strengthens the relationship between the benefactor and the beneficiary.

In conclusion, social media has brought about an unprecedented revolution in philanthropy. The golden age of digital philanthropy we are witnessing is marked by the complete transformation of the traditional constructs of giving. It has broken down barriers that traditionally characterized philanthropy - barriers of elitism, geographical limitations, lack of transparency, and trust. By providing a platform that is equally accessible and useful to all, social media has turned the power dynamics in philanthropy upside down, ushering in a new and more inclusive era for all. This is just the beginning of this fascinating evolution. As we delve deeper into the realm of viral philanthropy, hashtags, and social media campaigns, we will discover the full extent of these seismic shifts - a journey worth embarking on.

Chapter 4. Understanding the Power of Viral Philanthropy

In the current digital age, a novel method of supercharging philanthropic initiatives has evolved, leveraging the power of the internet and social media platforms that billions of individuals engage with daily. This chapter dives deep into the intricacies of viral philanthropy, its transformative potential, and a detailed analysis of the power dynamics that underpin this riveting phenomenon.

4.1. The Mechanics of Viral Philanthropy

Viral philanthropy is not just about randomly assigning charitable contributions over the web. It is a calculated, strategic method of channeling resources and aid towards distinct causes, amplified exponentially by the sharing mechanisms endemic to social media. The core of viral philanthropy lies distinctly in two key concepts: the viral coefficient and network externalities.

The viral coefficient is essentially the number of new users an existing user can bring to a platform. It measures the application's inherent virality, dictating the success of charity campaigns. In the context of viral philanthropy, a high viral coefficient leads to increased visibility of a philanthropic cause, raising awareness and subsequently contributing to its potential success.

On the other hand, network externalities describe the increase in the value of a good or service when its usage extends to more people. In the case of philanthropic campaigns shared over social media, each act of sharing adds value to the campaign in terms of extended reach and increased potential donations. Both these concepts, when combined, form the recipe for instantaneously reaching a wide audience, spurring organic and often exponential participation – the true mark of viral philanthropy.

4.2. The Transformative Influence of Viral Philanthropy

Social media's role in magnifying the impact of viral philanthropy cannot be overstated. Social media platforms render borderless outreach, amplifying messages across different geographies and demographics. Furthermore, they provide the ability to share real-time progress of campaigns, thereby instilling trust and facilitating user interaction and engagement.

The power of viral philanthropy also rests in its ability to evoke empathy propelled by compelling storytelling. Coupled with the tremendous reach of social media, these personalised narratives contribute to establishing emotional connections with potential donors regardless of geographical limitations.

Moreover, it empowers the ordinary citizen. You no longer need to be a billionaire or own a large corporation to make a real impact. With social media platforms and viral philanthropy, anyone can champion a cause, raise awareness, and marshal resources. This democratization of giving fosters inclusivity, thereby reshaping philanthropy.

4.3. Critique of Viral Philanthropy

While the power and potential of viral philanthropy are unmistakable, the concept isn't immune to criticism. Critics point out that while viral campaigns often result in an influx of donations, these sudden and large monetary contributions can sometimes overwhelm small organizations, adding strain on the management and allocation of the resources.

There's also the risk of 'slacktivism,' a phenomenon where people feel satisfied by merely sharing or liking a post associated with a cause, leading to negligible real-world participation or financial contributions. Having said this, it remains essential to note that even these criticisms can't diminish the disruptive potential of viral philanthropy which, when mobilized correctly, has the capacity to bring about significant social change.

4.4. Harnessing Viral Philanthropy: Best Practices

Knowing the power of viral philanthropy is one aspect; harnessing that power is another. It rests on several best practices, including storytelling, meticulous planning, and leveraging influencers. Effective storytelling encapsulates the essence of your cause, striking a chord with individuals and persuading them to donate. Planning involves understanding the audience and parsing through relevant metrics to optimize reach and engagement. Lastly, influencers offer a unique opportunity to amplify messages and drive virality; their endorsement can buoy a cause substantially.

The essence of viral philanthropy lies in its strategic utilization. It is not just a digitized broadcast of philanthropic messages but rather an exercise in smart media utilization. It maximizes the potential of every dollar donated and makes charity more efficient, inclusive, and impactful than ever before.

With its transformative potential, viral philanthropy is redefining the dynamics of social giving, breaking geographical, societal, and financial barriers. By unlocking the novel gates of digital giving, it's ensuring that the future of philanthropy is brimming with equal opportunities for all. The understanding and correctly simulating the power of viral philanthropy can not only redefine how we perceive charity but also vastly sustain the momentum needed to keep pushing the needle towards a more empathetic and supportive global society.

Chapter 5. The Role of Hashtags and Causes

In understanding the role of hashtags and causes in the philanthropic sphere, it is important to ponder on the power of these small yet influential symbols in today's digital age. They operate as a beacon, uniting worldwide sentiments under a common ideogram, and sparking conversations that traverse geographical boundaries to radiate a powerful impact on the global culture of philanthropy. From rallying support for a cause to crafting awareness campaigns, these hashtags set the rhythm of the charitable world's engagement with the public.

5.1. A Beacon of Unity

The hashtag, often prefixed to a word or phrase without spaces, stimulates connection and interaction on social media platforms. Its role in unitifying global conversations is exemplary. A hashtag tied to a philanthropic cause or mission, for instance, #CleanWaterForAll or #EducationMatters, encapsulates an idea, an initiative, or a pledge that various users around the world can get behind. These hashtags enable an international community of supporters to gather in one virtual space, sharing stories, experiences, and actions related to the cause. In essence, the hashtag is not merely a conduit for conversation—it is a fulcrum around which narratives of need, hope, and impact coalesce.

5.2. The Power of Viral Hashtags

A powerful hashtag has the potential to 'go viral,' its proliferation spurred by its resonance with a broad user base. Success stories of viral philanthropic campaigns commonly involve evocative hashtags. The #IceBucketChallenge for ALS awareness, the #NoMakeUpSelfie for cancer research, and #BlackLivesMatter for racial justice are just a few instances that testify to the potential of hashtags to rally global communities and generate a cascade of support and funding. The virality is, in part, a function of the community's deep involvement and emotional attachment to the cause. The stronger the emotional appeal, the more likely is the hashtag to spread, catalyzing conversation, action, and donations.

5.3. From Awareness to Action

Notably, beyond raising awareness and garnering likes or shares, the transformative power of hashtag philanthropy lies in its ability to spur tangible action. It crystalizes a social issue into a palatable and relatable concept, encouraging empathy, understanding, and, ultimately, action. Hashtags like #DonateNow or #TimeToAct, when tagged alongside those representing specific causes, underpin urgent call-to-actions. Recognizing the ability of the audience to drive change, these call-to-action hashtags induce a sense of urgency and responsibility, fostering a favorable environment for donations, volunteer sign-ups, and other forms of tangible assistance.

5.4. Navigating Hashtag Challenges

While the influence of hashtags is undeniable, it's not devoid of challenges. On one hand, the brevity of hashtags poses the risk of oversimplifying complex issues. Oversimplification could dilute the real essence of a cause, inhibiting nuanced discussions or fostering misunderstandings. On the other hand, the clutter of hashtags, owing to their ubiquitous usage, could potentially overshadow a cause or dilute its impact. To navigate such intricacies, it is essential to be strategic: use a unique and memorable hashtag, maintain consistency across all platforms, and ensure it resonates with the target audience and accurately conveys the nature of the cause.

5.5. Hashtags and Analytics

Finally, in the sea of hashtag philanthropy, assessing the reach and impact of a campaign necessitates the use of social media analytics. Tracking the trajectory of a hashtag – its mentions, impressions, and engagements – allows organizations to gauge campaign effectiveness, understand user behavior, and identify patterns and trends. Data extracted through hashtags also enables organizations to refine their messaging, identify key influencers, and enhance audience engagement, thereby amplifying their social impact.

In conclusion, hashtags, when leveraged effectively, serve as powerful tools for philanthropic causes to reach out, engage, and mobilize a global digital community. They drive unity, promote viral campaigns, facilitate action, and enable measurement of digital influence, thereby playing an instrumental role in shaping the future of philanthropy in today's social media landscape.

Chapter 6. Maximizing Engagement: The Art and Science of Social Media Campaigns

The intriguing sphere of philanthropy is rapidly morphing under the transformative influence of social media. A significant factor contributing to this dynamic shift is the utilization of social media campaigns with ingenious strategies that amplify engagement. The thrill of designing, implementing, and observing successful social media campaigns lies in recognizing the interplay between the art of human psychology and the science of data analytics.

6.1. The Art of Engagement

The essence of engagement in social media campaigns is, at its core, about persuasion and capturing the attention in a crowded digital landscape. To do this effectively, brands and philanthropic institutions tap into the universal human elements that bind us: storytelling, emotions, social validation, and a sense of belonging.

1. Storytelling is an ancient art form. It's a fundamental way humans have been sharing knowledge, passing on values and forging connections between individuals and communities. Skillfully integrating authentic and captivating narratives creates emotional resonance with the audience, and the philanthropic cause becomes a part of that individual's story. Telling stories of real people and their lived experiences amidst challenges makes the cause relatable, thereby fostering empathy and a drive to contribute to the cause.

2. Emotion serves as the catalyst to action. It has been said, "People

don't always remember what you say or do, but they always remember how you made them feel." After all, if the heart is not moved, the hands will not move.

3. Social proof plays a significant role in decision-making. As social animals, we humans tend to herd together, and seeing others take action encourages us to do the same. Philanthropic social media campaigns that highlight the collective participation of a community can drive individual actions effectively.

4. The human desire to belong is deeply ingrained. Engaging social media campaigns create an environment online that facilitates a sense of belonging among the participants. They feel they are part of a movement, a community that is effecting change.

6.2. Harnessing the Power of Social Media Tools

Notably, social media platforms offer a myriad of tools designed to drive interaction and engagement, making them indispensable for both strategizing and executing campaigns.

1. Live Streams: Both Facebook and Instagram have live streaming capabilities which can be used to host fundraising events or Q&A sessions that directly engage the audience with the cause or the people impacted by it.

2. Polls and Surveys: These tools offer an interactive way to gauge the sentiment of the audience while also collecting useful data that can feed into campaign strategies.

3. User Generated Content: Requesting and showcasing content from the audience builds a digital community around the cause, brings uniqueness to the campaign and promotes authenticity.

6.3. The Science of Engagement: Optimization Through Analytics

As important as the creativity of art in developing campaigns, the science of engagement lies in leveraging data to predict and optimize campaign performance.

Social media platforms offer extensive analytics capabilities to track an array of metrics such as likes, shares, comments, impressions, reach, and click-through rates. These provide critical insight into audience behavior and campaign effectiveness.

Studying these metrics allows organizations to evaluate the performance of their campaign and fine-tune strategies based on user feedback. A/B tests can be conducted to experiment with different types of content, headlines, or timing to observe what achieves the most traction with the audience.

6.4. Devising the Ideal Social Media Philanthropy Campaign

Devising an ideal social media campaign for philanthropic purposes is an iterative process that begins with clear goals and objectives and then evolves based on audience feedback and engagement analysis.

A winning campaign begins by identifying target demographics, designing tailored content that aligns with their preferences, scheduling posts for peak engagement times, and engaging in consistent, meaningful interaction with followers.

Through these methods, campaigns can achieve a multiplier effect, not only in terms of increased donations but also greater awareness, heightened community involvement, improved perception of the organization, and an overall advance toward the goal of creating a more compassionate and caring world.

To conclude, the art and science of social media campaigns in the context of philanthropy embodies a strategic game plan woven with compelling narratives, psychological triggers, and evidence-based decision-making. In this transformative age, social media serves as a powerful tool to maximize engagement and uplift the cause of philanthropy.

Chapter 7. Influencers and Celebrities Unleashing Philanthropy 2.0

In an era where digital media has the power to shake up longstanding structures and challenge traditional norms, the roles of influencers and celebrities are significantly evolving. Their impacts are not limited to mere product endorsements or advertising campaigns; instead, their reach extends to new landscapes, particularly the field of philanthropy. This remarkable shift, self-dubbed as 'Philanthropy 2.0', is dissected in detail in the following sections.

7.1. A New Breed of Philanthropy

Philanthropy as we know it is going through a significant metamorphosis brought on by the digital wave, notably characterized by the advent of influencers and celebrities steering this wave of change. Influencers and celebrities often have large followings extending to millions - or in some cases, even tens of hundreds of millions. They are using their considerable sway to support, advocate, and fundraise for vital causes, pushing forward a distinctive form of philanthropy, now popularly known as 'Philanthropy 2.0'.

Philanthropy 2.0 is a new breed of charitable giving that harnesses the immense penetration and influence of digital personalities to motivate change. It embraces a more direct and involved approach, seeking not just to generate financial support but to also cultivate a culture of involved giving. The characteristics of this nascent paradigm are diverse and multi-dimensional, adjusted and formed in response to the powerful influence of social media.

7.2. Impact of Influencer-Driven Philanthropy

Influencer-driven philanthropy is creating a ripple effect of change in society. This impact is multi-layered and works essentially on two fronts: first, it empowers causes by promoting them to a vast potential audience; second, it motivates others, particularly the younger cohorts, to get involved in philanthropic activity. In essence, influencers and celebrities are redefining philanthropy by promoting a more democratized, participatory, and accessible system of charitable actions.

This democratization of philanthropy has fundamentally interrupted the dynamics of charitable giving. By lending their voices to social causes and turning the spotlight onto significant issues, influencers allow their audience to feel comfortable engaging with typically under-discussed topics.

7.3. Case Studies: Influencers Shaping Philanthropy 2.0

To better understand the role of influencers in reshaping philanthropy, we shall delve into a few poignant examples. The infamous ALS Ice Bucket Challenge is one of the earliest instances where celebrities played a significant role in encouraging social participation. This viral campaign, borne out of an imaginative idea and propelled by influencers and celebrities alike, managed to raise around $115 million in donations for ALS research.

Another powerful illustration comes from British YouTuber, Zoe 'Zoella' Sugg, who leveraged her online platform to raise awareness about mental health issues. Through candid videos discussing her struggles, Zoe demystified mental health conversations and encouraged her following to support various relevant charities.

On the cusp of mega-stardom and influence, US-based singer-songwriter Taylor Swift has continually demonstrated remarkable commitment towards charitable causes. Swift is known to utilize her vast social media presence to draw attention to and donate towards calamity-stricken areas, children's hospitals, or education funds.

7.4. The Awesome Force of Celebrities in Philanthropy

Equivalent to influencers, celebrities too have a unique role to play in this 'Philanthropy 2.0' era. They typically bring along a significant mass appeal and extensive visibility. In our increasingly socially conscious world, many admirers look up to celebrities not just for entertainment but also for their advocacy work. When celebrities get involved in philanthropy work, they offer a compelling narrative that strikes a chord with their fans, on a much larger scale.

Take the example of Angelina Jolie. Beyond her Hollywood fame, she is known for her humanitarian work. Jolie has been a UNHCR Goodwill Ambassador since 2001 and has visited numerous humanitarian hotspots around the world. Her hands-on approach to philanthropy, be it donating her time, resources, or sponsoring various initiatives, has been instrumental in offering aid and awareness to a multitude of causes. Her philanthropic methods admirably embody the spirit of Philanthropy 2.0.

7.5. Analytics: Understanding the Impact

In the world of 'Philanthropy 2.0', the assessment of influence extends beyond mere retweets and likes. It is crucial to discern the quality of engagement – are the posts prompting a healthy discussion? Are viewers moved to action? Are the campaigns leading to quantifiable changes?

Take, for instance, a study done by Twitter which revealed that social justice-related hashtags spiked dramatically in 2020. While this increase was due partly to heightened global incidents, it was equally a testament to powerful social influencers and celebrities championing social causes.

7.6. Going Forward

As we tread further into this brave new world of 'Philanthropy 2.0,' influencers and celebrities are set to become even more instrumental in reshaping the realm of charitable giving. This transformation will depend on their ability to construct authentic connections and engage with their audience on issues that truly matter. With the rise of conscious consumership and social activism, the partnership between social media and philanthropy has become an unstoppable force, promising a future that is much more equitable and compassionate. In a nutshell, this symbiosis is indeed creating a philanthropic landscape that is as inspiring as it is formidable.

Chapter 8. Real-World Cases of Viral Philanthropy: Success Stories and Lessons

In the vortex of social media, numerous cases of viral philanthropic campaigns have left indelible marks on the global conscience. These success stories of viral philanthropy illuminate the possibilities and potential pitfalls in leveraging social media for charitable causes, and indeed, they merit a deep dive for the promise they hold in sketching the future of philanthropy.

8.1. Viral Sensations: #nomakeupselfie and the Ice Bucket Challenge

Groundbreaking campaigns have emerged from the ever-evolving, boundary-pushing conveniences of our modern, digitally-connected world. While virality is an unpredictable recipe, it's undeniable that the #nomakeupselfie campaign and the ALS Ice Bucket Challenge are two phenomenal social media occurrences that showcased the potential of viral philanthropy.

The #nomakeupselfie campaign, an organic, user-generated social media tidal wave, encouraged women to post their bare-faced selfies online in a symbolic display of solidarity and awareness for cancer research charities. What followed was a stunning, thoroughly digital, collective endeavor, with millions of women from around the globe participating and donating to cancer research charities. This unanticipated trend raised over £8 million ($10.4 million) in just six days for Cancer Research UK, creating a global shift in understanding the merits of social media-infused philanthropy.

Similarly, the ALS Ice Bucket Challenge launched in 2014 and rapidly transformed into a digital wildfire. This was a simple, fun, and participatory campaign that doused the internet, viewing millions of people worldwide get drenched and challenge their friends and family to do the same or donate to support ALS research. It raised over $115 million for the ALS Association and exponentially increased awareness of the disease, leading to significant research breakthroughs.

8.2. Stars Galore: Red Nose Day

Celebrities becoming philanthropists isn't new, but the marriage of their influence and social media in driving philanthropic causes is a unique phenomenon brought forth by this digital era. One of the profound examples of this is Red Nose Day. Initiated by the British charity Comic Relief in 1988 and thence carried overseas, Red Nose Day is a biennial fundraising telethon that's taken to social platforms with wild success. Celebrities upload silly photos on their Facebook, Twitter, Instagram, and Snapchat accounts, wearing goofy red noses to boost the campaign's reach. With the power of these big names and the appeal of social media, Red Nose Day has helped raise over $1 billion globally to combat child poverty.

8.3. The Unexpected Leap: From Disasters to Viral Aid

Sudden natural disasters often leave communities vulnerable, but the collective power of the online community has been crucial in assisting swift recovery. The Haiti earthquake in 2010 was perhaps the first instance of social media rallying immediately to respond to a disaster. Text-based donations proliferated, and many nonprofits and charities used Twitter and Facebook to mobilize aid, supplies, and volunteers. This instantaneous, humanity-based digital reaction demonstrated that even in dire circumstances, mobilizing social media can result in significant resource-generation, fostering a sense of global unity.

8.4. Overcoming Challenges: Viral Philanthropy Isn't Always a Victory

With virality comes increased scrutiny, greater responsibility, and often, challenges of varying sorts. For instance, while the ALS Ice Bucket Challenge was a significant victory, there were critiques around the awareness vs donation balance, environmental impact of water wastage, and concerns of overshadowing other nonprofit efforts.

Moreover, the "Kony 2012" campaign illustrates that social media can be a double-edged sword. It started as a compelling narrative aimed at capturing the war criminal Joseph Kony, pooling massive online engagement. However, it swiftly encountered backlash, mainly due to over-simplified narratives and misrepresentation of facts, presenting a crucial lesson about the responsibilities tied with crafting and circulating viral campaigns.

Understanding and learning from these real-world instances is integral to harnessing the capabilities of social media in philanthropy. Viral philanthropy's dynamic landscape offers a novel path for engaging individuals and enriching lives. Notwithstanding its challenges, the promise it holds is immense and exciting, representative of the symbiotic relationship between social media and philanthropy. As we step into this transformative era, it's up to us to leverage this potent partnership responsibly, ethically, and benefit the world at large.

Chapter 9. The Dark Side: Overcoming Challenges in Social Media and Philanthropy

The landscape of philanthropy is being transformed, with the evolution of social media at the center of this remarkable shift. However, like any potent tool, it comes with its own slew of potential challenges. Merging the realms of charity and social media promises enlightening prospects; however, it also holds some dark corners that need addressing. In this chapter, we will shine a light on these areas to understand how they can be effectively navigated and managed.

9.1. Challenges and Pitfalls of Social Media in Philanthropy

Social media, known for its immediacy, universality, and virality, is finding an increasingly synergistic relationship with philanthropy. Yet, the very same features can be the root of certain challenges. Social media platforms, though tremendous facilitators of outreach and engagement, can equally serve as fertile grounds for misinformation, scam campaigns, and even exacerbate existing socio-economic disparities.

For example, while the viral nature of social media can propel a philanthropic campaign to unprecedented heights, the speed and reach of these viral incidents can sometimes outpace verification processes. Fake campaigns and charity scams can easily gain traction. High-profile cases like the 2012 Kony campaign underscore the dangers of fast-spreading but poorly researched initiatives.

Further compounding this issue is the risk of "slacktivism," a term used to define low-effort, feel-good activities that often do little to effect significant change. The simplicity of sharing a post or adding a hashtag can create an illusion of impact, without translating into meaningful action or financial support.

9.2. Overcoming Challenges and Shaping a Healthier Philanthropic Ecosystem

However, these challenges should not overshadow the potential of social media as a tool for philanthropy but motivate us to develop proper strategies to mitigate them.

One approach is to educate stakeholders about the need to authenticate campaigns before sharing or contributing to them. Alongside this, social media platforms themselves need to strengthen their own verification processes to protect users from fraudulent campaigns.

Furthermore, fostering tangible actions beyond click-and-share can mitigate the risks of slacktivism. Nonprofits can design campaigns that encourage deeper engagement, such as volunteering, starting conversations around the cause, or even running peer-to-peer fundraising initiatives.

9.3. Consequences of Ignoring Ethical Considerations

Ignoring such considerations can have grave implications. Ethical challenges such as invasion of privacy, undue influence, and enhanced exposure to aggressive marketing tactics can arise if ignored. Ensuring informed consent and protecting data privacy should be prioritized in order to maintain credibility and trust.

Moreover, an often overlooked aspect is how social media can unintentionally worsen the digital divide between different demographics. If not strategically managed, such divisions can ultimately undermine the essence of inclusivity that philanthropy seeks to promote.

9.4. Respecting the Digital Divide in Philanthropy

To maintain an inclusive and equitable philanthropic landscape, we need to remember that access to social media is far from universal. The internet and digital technologies remain out of reach for a significant proportion of people globally. By over-relying on online platforms for philanthropy, there's a risk of excluding these individuals and communities from the process of giving and receiving.

Balancing online campaigns with traditional philanthropic methods and considering partnerships with organizations that can bridge this gap are some practices that should be considered.

9.5. Incorporating the Lessons and Preparing for the Future

Cognizant of these challenges and equipped with action plans to address them, social media philanthropy can continue to be a powerful driving force for change. By acknowledging the dark side, we are made aware of the potential pitfalls on our pathway to positive societal impact. All efforts in overcoming these challenges, therefore, bring us closer to our goal of creating a healthier philanthropic ecosystem in this interwoven world of social media and philanthropy. By adopting an attitude of compassion, adaptability, and commitment to continuous learning, we can ensure the integrity and authenticity of our philanthropic endeavors on social media.

This chapter underlines the fact that while the crossroads of social media and philanthropy can indeed be a match made in heaven, it requires careful, conscious navigation to ensure that this promising relationship is beneficial for all involved. Let's continue examining the trailblazing marriage of social media and philanthropy as we delve into its impact and future potential in the following chapters.

Chapter 10. Measuring the Impact of Social Philanthropy: Analytics and Identity

Understanding the impact of social philanthropy has become an increasingly pivotal aspect of leveraging the power of social media for charitable endeavors. Essentially, it's about striking a balance between analytics and identity to formulate a coherent and concise understanding of outreach, efficacy, and the broader implications of a given charitable initiative.

10.1. The Significance of Analytics in Social Philanthropy

Analytics in social philanthropy essentially concern the quantification of critical data related to philanthropic initiatives in social media landscapes. They provide tangible metrics for assessing effectiveness, optimizing execution, and substantiating the overall impacts of social philanthropy efforts.

Crucially, these dynamic tools measure results, monitor trends, predict outcomes and help in making data-driven decisions, thereby equipping philanthropists with a nuanced understanding of the operational landscape. Variables such as reach, impressions, engagements, click-through rates, donation amounts, and conversion rates become essential indicators of performance and aids in strategy formulation.

10.2. Identity - The Human Element in Measuring Impact

While analytics presents the quantifiable aspect of measuring impact, identity—understood as the broader socio-cultural repercussions of a philanthropic initiative—provides a more qualitative measure. This includes questions around which demographics are most responsive, to whom the charitable activities significantly impact, and how those communities are expressing their experiences and perceptions on social platforms.

This nuanced understanding makes identity an indispensable metric, breathing life into the skeletal data points and transforming the statistics into stories. Moreover, recognizing this human element factors into building reputation, cultivating trust, and fostering a sense of community among donors, volunteers, and beneficiaries.

10.3. Interplay between Analytics and Identity: A Holistic Approach

Both analytics and identity are equally intrinsic to assessing the impact of social philanthropy. Hence, measuring them collectively gives a more holistic projection of the effectiveness of endeavors. Using analytics to derive patterns in behavioral data, backed by identity insights, can paint a vivid picture of the social dynamics at play within philanthropic initiatives.

Optimizing one's philanthropic strategies becomes easier and more effective when guided by this combined viewpoint. While analytics offer unequivocal data, the interpretive richness of identity analysis contributes to a more context-sensitive understanding of said data. This synergy, when tapped into diligently, can transform the way philanthropic strategies are built, implemented, and evaluated.

10.4. The Tools for Measurement: From Basic Metrics To Advanced Analytics

Measurement tools range from in-app analytics offered by various social platforms to advanced third-party analytics tools that provide deep dives into complex data. Basic metrics such as likes, shares, and followers on social media platforms are simple ways of tracking engagement.

Advanced analytics tools can provide insight into the donor's journey - from the first point of contact to the act of donating. They can track key performance indicators (KPIs) such as conversion rates, average donation amount, cost per acquisition, and others, enabling a close monitoring of campaign performance and driving data-based decisions. Various analytical models can also help predict future trends, thus aiding in strategic planning.

10.5. Challenges and Opportunities in Impact Measurement

Although the measurement of social philanthropy efforts seems inescapable in this digital age, it's not without challenges. The inherent volatility and complexity of social media platforms may lead to difficulties in accurately tracking data. Privacy concerns, fluctuating algorithms, and varying user behaviors may constrain the comprehensiveness and accuracy of the data being measured.

However, these challenges create rich opportunities for metric innovation, privacy advancement, and algorithmic transparency, which in turn may act as catalysts for future advances in the field. As the digital landscape continues to evolve, so too must the evaluation tools and methodologies employed in measuring the impact of social philanthropy.

Through this lens, each metric becomes more than just a number or a statistic. It becomes a testament to the transformative synergy of social media and philanthropy, opening eyes and affecting real-world change in the realm of philanthropy. In the words of philanthropy tycoon, Andrew Carnegie, the "man who dies rich dies disgraced." Social media and philanthropy allow us all an opportunity to leverage our collective wealth—be it monetary, influencer, or intellectual—to sculpt a better world.

Chapter 11. The Future of Philanthropy: Predictions and Preparations for What Lies Ahead

Bearing witness to the continuous unfolding of the landscape of philanthropy, we find ourselves at the threshold of a future filled with a myriad of exciting possibilities. Hampered by conventional means and methodology for centuries, philanthropy is experiencing a seismic shift, primarily driven by the potent power of social media. As we scrutinize emerging trends and extrapolate, observe the future trajectories, and mentally prepare for what's to come, it becomes apparent that the interplay between philanthropy and social media is poised to herald a revolutionary era. Staring ahead at the path waiting to be tread, one is overtaken by a sense of awe and keen anticipation of the wonders the future of philanthropy promises.

11.1. The Age of Hyper-Connectivity and Philanthropy

In an era marked by hyper-connectivity and instant communications, the philanthropic landscape is evolving at an unprecedented pace. The power of social media platforms to reach a broad, global audience is having a transformative effect on philanthropy, challenging traditional norms while simultaneously carving new paths of communal good. Going forward, the diverse range of digital tools will continue to play a formative role. Moreover, as augmented and virtual realities become more mainstream, the charitable sector will have even more innovative avenues to engage donors and rally their support, creating an immersive philanthropic experience that transcends geographical borders.

11.2. Democratisation of Philanthropy

Historically, philanthropic efforts were concentrated in the hands of a select few - wealthy individuals, generous families, or grand multi-million dollar foundations. But as we step into the horizon of this new era, we foresee a landscape where philanthropy becomes even more widespread and commonplace, largely attributed to the democratising impact of social media. Crowdfunding campaigns, grassroots activism, micro-donations – these elements, by the virtue of social media, are set to make everyone a philanthropist, pooling resources in an unprecedented collective effort to make the world a better place.

11.3. Social Philanthropy and The Rise of Conscious Capitalism

Amidst the transformation of philanthropy, there is a dawning recognition of the connection between business and charity. Social entrepreneurship and conscious capitalism are on the rise, and businesses are discovering that profitable practices and philanthropy are not mutually exclusive but rather can and should coexist. Organisations are beginning to witness the power of social media to display their corporate responsibility initiatives, ushering in an era of publically accountable, transparent, and socially-conscious corporates.

11.4. The Challenge of Ensuring Authenticity and Overcoming Digital Fatigue

While the power of social media in reshaping philanthropy cannot be understated, it is equally crucial to acknowledge the challenges that loom ahead. The widespread use and at times misuse of social media bring forward the issue of authenticity. Therefore, it will become crucially important for organisations to work towards establishing trust with the online community. Furthermore, they will need to strategize to overcome potential digital fatigue among users, ensuring that essential messages of philanthropy don't get lost in the overflow of digital content.

11.5. The Indispensable Role of Analytics

As social media continues to reshape the future of philanthropy, the role of analytics will become increasingly significant. Metrics underscoring reach, engagement, and impact will be vital to understanding and improving philanthropic efforts. Harnessing the bristling potential of AI and machine learning, social media platforms will generate insightful data that would serve as the bedrock for driving effective and impactful philanthropic strategies.

Finally, we set sight on the role of youth in steering this shift. Tomorrow's leaders are today's digital natives, whose familiarity with social media and comfort with the digital world make them the likely torchbearers for this transformation. Coupled with their genuine desire to make a difference, and guided by the wisdom of experienced practitioners, they will lead the way, ensuring the future of philanthropy is as promising as it is exciting.

We're on the cusp of an extraordinary future for philanthropy. Driven by the transformative engine of social media and fuelled by a global online community committed to positive change, the future of philanthropy is teeming with promise, ensuring a legacy of better, fairer, and more compassionate world.